A Book of Courage

101 Quotes for Cultivating a Courageous Mindset

Dedication

If you bought this for someone, write something nice about them here. If you bought this for yourself, write something nice about you here. If you want to write something about the book, scan the QR code below to leave a review.

Leave a review → → → → →

Author's Note

Welcome to my book of courage. These quotes have been collated by me over the years as I have worked to overcome adversity, achieve my dreams and stand up to speak up. It started with a handwritten list which kept growing as I kept challenging myself to push my own boundaries. As my list grew, I knew it was time to bring my courage to the digital age. I decided to turn it into a book so that I could carry it with me wherever I go, and share it with others who may also need a little pep talk from time to time.

Fear is inevitable and is actually an important survival mechanism. It serves as a valuable warning system, enabling us to take appropriate action to ensure our safety. Fear can also be exploited to deliberately manipulate and control others. The problem is that it all feels the same. As Plato said, "Courage is knowing what not to fear". And therein lies the challenge.

Fears come in all shapes and sizes. Courage is required in many different forms for different reasons. One philosophy or quote can't encapsulate all the wisdom required to grow all types of courage. It takes a strong person to acknowledge their fears and seek out the motivation to overcome them. In fact, some of the greatest leaders and visionaries of our time have relied on the power of inspiring quotes and philosophies to keep them going. This book is a testament to that.

These quotes are my personal favorites, straight from the mouths of people who've been there, done that, and have the scars to prove it. They remind me that before anyone becomes successful, they need courage first. When it comes to finding the courage to overcome our fears, it's important to remember that we are only human, and it's okay to have moments of doubt and fear. In fact, it's perfectly normal. I re-read my list of courage quotes when I need to reignite the fire within to pursue my dreams.

And you, my friend, have that courage within you. It takes guts to believe in yourself and see your own greatness, especially in the face of opposition where it's so much easier to focus on the negative. But with this book, you will be inspired to see just how much you are capable of overcoming.

Remember that courage comes from within, and no one can give it to you. We all have to build our own foundations of strength, and that takes courage. The quotes in this book are living proof that people throughout history, from all walks of life, have exercised great courage to become the successful and influential individuals of today. Building courage isn't only about changing the world or super achieving. Perhaps the biggest test of courage is simply being yourself, and living your best life according to your own standards.

It can also refer to having the bravery to pursue a new passion, start a new chapter in life, or even just take a step outside of your comfort zone.

A Book of Courage

Sometimes, it takes a lot of courage to let go of what's comfortable and embrace the unknown. Building courage means embracing the possibility of failure, but also the potential for incredible growth and learning. So let's not just focus on the tough, gritty side of courage. Let's also acknowledge the sunny, hopeful side of it, the side that pushes us towards new beginnings and exciting adventures.

This method has helped me in my life. I'm sharing my book of courage in the hopes it may help you practice believing in yourself.

101 Quotes for Cultivating a Courageous Mindset

In no particular order

"Courage is resistance to fear, mastery of fear, not absence of fear."

- *Mark Twain*

"Fear is a reaction. Courage is a decision."

- *Winston Churchill*

"It's better to be a lion for a day than a sheep all your life."

- *Elizabeth Kenny*

"Be brave. Take risks. Nothing can substitute experience."

- *Paulo Coelho*

"The greatest test of courage on the earth is to bear defeat without losing heart."

- *Robert Green Ingersoll*

"Courage is the magic that turns dreams into reality."

- Aberjhani

"A ship is safe in harbor but that's not what ships are for."

- John A. Shedd

"Courage is being scared to death and saddling up anyway."

- *John Wayne*

"Are you feeling a bit shaken, maybe stirred, maybe fearful and doubtful and completely utterly wildly terrified? Good. Keep going."

- *Victoria Erickson*

"You were born of the stars dear one; stop settling for the dust they leave behind."

- *Lang Leav*

"You never know how strong you are until being strong is the only choice you have."

- *Bob Marley*

"If you want something you've never had you have to do something you've never done. Freedom lies in being bold."

- Coco Chanel

"You can't be brave if you've only had wonderful things happen to you."

- *Mary Tyler Moore*

"And by the way, everything in life is writable about if you have the outgoing guts to do it and the imagination to improvise. The worst enemy to creativity is self-doubt."

- *Sylvia Plath*

"When one's mind is made up this diminishes fear; knowing what must be done does away with fear."

- *Rosa Parks*

"Sometimes the smallest step in the right direction ends up being the biggest step of your life. Tiptoe if you must, but take the step."

- *Naeem Callaway*

"Strength does not come from physical capacity. It comes from an indomitable will."

- *Mahatma Gandhi*

"You must do the thing you think you cannot do."

- Eleanor Roosevelt.

"Courage is the power to let go of the familiar."

- *Raymond Lindquist*

"Courage is the discovery that you may not win, and trying when you know you can lose."

- *Tom Krause*

"Man cannot discover new oceans unless he has the courage to lose sight of the shore."

- *André Gide*

"Courage is the art of being the only one who knows you're scared to death."

- *Harold Wilson*

"Life shrinks or expands in proportion to one's courage."

- Anaïs Nin

"It's not the size of the dog in the fight, it's the size of the fight in the dog."

- *Mark Twain*

"The only limit to our realization of tomorrow will be our doubts of today."

- *Franklin D. Roosevelt*

"Courage is the price that life exacts for granting peace."

- *Amelia Earhart*

"You are worn and cracked and dented. And that is okay, because I have never heard of a clean and shiny sword that won a war."

- Erin van Vuren

"Courage isn't the strength to go on – it is going on when you don't have strength."

- *Napoleon Bonaparte*

"A man with outward courage dares to die; a man with inner courage dares to live."

- *Lao Tzu*

"True courage is like a kite: a contrary wind raises it higher."

- *John Petit-Senn*

"Courage is the commitment to begin without any guarantee of success."

- *Marianne Williamson*

"Be fearless in the pursuit of what sets your soul on fire."

- *Jennifer Lee*

"It's easy to be brave from a safe distance."

- *Louisa May Alcott*

"Courage is the most important of all the virtues because without courage, you can't practice any other virtue consistently. We can't be kind, true, merciful, generous or honest."

- Maya Angelou

"Few persons have courage enough to appear as good as they really are."

- *Charles Lambs*

"It takes courage
to believe the
best is yet to
come."

- Julia Roberts

"Stars can't shine without darkness."

- *D.H. Sidebottom*

"Courage doesn't mean you don't get afraid. Courage means you don't let fear stop you."

- Bethany Hamilton

"The greatest glory in living lies not in never falling, but in rising every time we fall."

- Nelson Mandela

"All our dreams can come true if we have the courage to pursue them."

- *Walt Disney*

"It takes courage to grow up and become who you really are."

- *E.E. Cummings*

"Don't let the noise of other's opinions drown out your own inner voice. Have the courage to follow your heart and intuition. They somehow already know what you truly want."

- *Steve Jobs*

"It takes a great deal of bravery to stand up to our enemies, but just as much to stand up to our friends."

- *J.K. Rowling*

"Fairy tales are more than true; not because they tell us that dragons exist, but because they tell us that dragons can be beaten."

- G.K Chesterton

"You gain strength, courage and confidence by every experience in which you really stop to look fear in the face."

- Eleanor Roosevelt

"The world is in a constant conspiracy against the brave. It's the age-old struggle: the roar of the crowd on the one side, and the voice of your conscience on the other."

- *Pierre Teilhard de Chardin*

"Wrong is wrong, even if everyone is doing it. Right is right, even if no one is doing it."

- *St. Augustine of Hippo*

"The opposite of courage is not cowardice, it is conformity. Even a dead fish can go with the flow."

- Jim Hightower

"True courage is not the brutal force of vulgar heroes, but the firm resolve of virtue and reason."

- *Alfred North Whitehead*

"Courage is fire, and bullying is smoke."

- *Benjamin Disraeli*

"Faced with what is right, to leave it undone shows a lack of courage."

- *Confucius*

"Every man has his own courage, and is betrayed because he seeks in himself the courage of other persons."

- Ralph Waldo Emerson

"The most courageous act is still to think for yourself. Aloud."

- *Coco Chanel*

"You may never know what results come of your actions, but if you do nothing, there will be no results."

- Mahatma Gandhi

"God grants me the courage not to give up what I think is right even though I think it is hopeless."

- Chester W. Nimitz

"The brave may not live forever, but the cautious don't live at all."

- *Richard Branson*

"Whenever you find yourself doubting how far you can go, just remember how far you have come. Remember everything you have faced, all the battles you have won, and all the fears you have overcome."

- N.R. Walker

"Believe you can and you're halfway there."

- *Theodore Roosevelt*

"Courage doesn't always roar. Sometimes courage is the quiet voice at the end of the day saying, 'I will try again tomorrow."

- Mary Anne Radmacher

"You are under the unfortunate impression that just because you run away you have no courage."

- Cowardly Lion, from "The Wonderful Wizard of Oz" by L. Frank Baum

"Knowing when to walk away is wisdom. Being able to is courage. Walking away with your head held high is dignity."

- *Ritu Ghatourey*

"Courage is looking fear right in the eye and saying - Get the hell out of my way, I've got things to do."

- *Anonymous*

"You are strong enough to face it all, even if it doesn't feel like it right now."

- *Marianne Williamson*

"Courage is going from one failure to another with no loss of enthusiasm."

- *Winston Churchill*

"What you are afraid to do is a clear indication of the next thing you need to do."

- *Ralph Waldo Emerson*

"Never let the fear of striking out get in your way."

- *Babe Ruth*

"Just as courage is the danger of life, so is fear its safeguard."

- *Leonardo Da Vinci*

"What good are wings without the courage to fly?"

- *Atticus*

"Courage is a
love affair with
the unknown."

- *Osho*

"You can't test courage cautiously."

- *Annie Dillard*

"You can choose courage or you can choose comfort, but you cannot choose both."

- *Brené Brown*

"Do one thing every day that scares you."

- *Eleanor Roosevelt*

"Courage is grace under pressure."

- *Ernest Hemingway*

"Without courage, wisdom bears no fruit."

- *Baltasar Gracian*

"The courage to be is the courage to accept oneself, in spite of being unacceptable."

- *Paul Tillichs*

"With enough courage, you can do without a reputation."

- *Margaret Mitchell*

"Courage is very important. Like a muscle, it is strengthened by use."

- *Ruth Gordon*

"He who is not courageous enough to take risks will accomplish nothing in life."

- *Muhammad Ali*

"Courage is contagious. When a brave man takes a stand, the spines of others are often stiffened."

- *Billy Graham*

"Courage is not the absence of fear, but rather the assessment that something else is more important than fear."

- Franklin D. Roosevelt

"It takes a lot of courage to show your dreams to someone else."

- *Erma Bombeck*

"We must build dikes of courage to hold back the flood of fear."

- Martin Luther King, Jr

"Being deeply loved by someone gives you strength, while loving someone deeply gives you courage."

- Lao Tzu

"Have the courage to act instead of react."

- *Oliver Wendell Holmes*

"Failure is unimportant. It takes courage to make a fool of yourself."

- *Charlie Chaplin*

"Mistakes are always forgivable, if one has the courage to admit them."

- *Bruce Lee*

"If you have the courage to begin, you have the courage to succeed."

- Harry Hoover

"Courage is what it takes to stand up and speak; courage is also what it takes to sit down and listen."

- *Winston Churchill*

"People with courage and character always seem sinister to the rest."

- *Hermann Hesse*

"Life is mostly froth and bubble. Two things stand like stone. Kindness in another's trouble, Courage in your own."

- Adam Lindsay Gordon

"Believe in yourself. You are braver than you think, more talented than you know, and capable of more than you imagine."

- *Roy T. Bennett*

"Without fear, there cannot be courage."

- *Christopher Paolini*

"There is a stubbornness about me that never can bear to be frightened at the will of others. My courage always rises at every attempt to intimidate me."

- *Jane Austen*

"Everyone has talent. What's rare is the courage to follow it to the dark places where it leads."

- *Erica Jong*

"Courage results when one's convictions are bigger than one's fears."

- *Orrin Woodward*

"Don't be afraid of your fears. They're not there to scare you. They're there to let you know that something is worth it."

- *C. JoyBell C.*

"Have enough courage to trust love one more time and always one more time."

- Maya Angelou

"Jump, and you will find out how to unfold your wings as you fall."

- *Ray Bradbury*

"He who jumps into the void owes no explanation to those who stand and watch."

- *Jean-Luc Godard*

"Those who lack the courage will always find a philosophy to justify it."

- *Albert Camus*

Fate whispers to the warrior, "You cannot withstand the storm." The warrior whispers back, "I am the storm."

- *Genghis Khan*

Parting Thought:

"The best revenge is none. Heal, move on and don't become like those who hurt you."

- *Pamela Short*

13802820R00072